LONDON'S LAST
ROUTEMASTERS

Capital Transport

INSIDE

JAMES LIDSEY

FRONT COVER
CAPITAL TRANSPORT

BACK COVER
PHILIPPA SPRATT

TITLE PAGE
CAPITAL TRANSPORT

BACK PAGE
MARK KEHOE

OPPOSITE
MARK KEHOE

CAPITAL TRANSPORT

London's Last Routemasters David Stewart

At the beginning of the 21st Century, it seemed that the Routemaster could survive in normal London service for another ten years or even longer. On 22nd September 2000 TfL announced that twenty-four RMs had been bought back. The press notice said that they were "to be put into service on existing Routemaster routes allowing refurbishment of existing buses to be carried out where necessary without causing disruption." It went on to affirm that "They are a practical solution for central London as well as good value. We can put three fully refurbished and modernised Routemasters on the road for the price of one brand new bus. They are popular for a variety of reasons, some people like having a conductor on board." TfL's Transport Strategy issued in July 2001 suggested that two thirds of central London double-deck routes were to have conductors by the end of 2004. The aims were to improve speed, reliability, personal security and accessibility. How things changed – and how quickly.

The initial batch of re-purchased RMs was duly refurbished by Marshall Bus of Cambridge, and the first example was on the road in June 2001. Route 13 was converted to the type, allowing RMLs to cover shortages elsewhere, with some indirectly replacing doored buses that were being used on crew routes because of insufficient Routemasters to go round. Eventually, forty-nine RMs were bought back, and Marshall Bus refurbished most of them.

Around 200 extra conductors were recruited, and many were used to restore several evening and Sunday services from driver-only back to crew operation, and to slightly increase a few frequencies. Between 31st March and 29th September 2001, routes 8, 13, 14, 19, 38, 94, 137 and 159 all regained Sunday Routemasters and conductors. The weekday peak vehicle requirement (pvr) for crew operation on Routemasters had been around the 500 mark for some years, indeed since the last crew to driver only conversion of route 139

4

on 28th March 1998. At early summer 2000, the pvr figure was 507. The small increases to pvrs, mainly during 2002, saw this figure rise inexorably in twos and threes to 530 by June 2002. The increase to services in central London in the run-up to Congestion Charging from February 2003 saw larger pvr rises in the latter half of 2002, peaking at 574 on 1st February 2003, the highest point since July 1992.

An indication of the aims in TfL's Transport Strategy came when one driver only route, the 55 from Leyton to Oxford Circus was converted back to conductor operation from 13th October 2001, but still utilising Tridents. It largely paralleled the 48 and was chosen partly to see if conductors helped to speed up boarding and journey times in comparison with the 48. This was seen as a positive attraction to car users who, it was thought, would be displaced to buses once Congesting Charging was introduced in February 2003. In the event, the difference between crew and one-person operation was insignificant, and the experiment was ended, the 55 reverting to driver-only operation from 4th January 2003.

Meanwhile, other things were beginning to become apparent in the fares and ticketing arena. The fares structure in London had been based on zones across the bus network but eventually ended up with simple flat cash fares. More and more passengers bought daily, weekly, monthly and annual Travelcards, whilst the uptake of Bus Passes and the new Savers increased. By 2004, the range of 'off bus ticketing' was expanded with Oyster Cards and a 'pre-pay' banked fare payment facility. The articulated buses on Red Arrow routes that arrived in summer 2002 had already introduced 'cash-less' operation. All passengers had to have a ticket before boarding, and ticket machines were installed at relevant stops in central London. A similar experiment was undertaken on route W8 in north London, and the idea soon spread to the whole of the West End on all routes and all types of bus. TfL expressed intentions to extend the cashless principle to the whole of the TfL area in due course. From April 2003 men between the ages of 60 and 65 were brought into the Freedom Pass scheme, already wheelchair users and certain disabled people received free off-peak travel, whilst in summer 2005 further controversial initiatives allowed more children to travel free. With the number of passengers holding pre-purchased, concessionary or free tickets or passes, boarding times were becoming ever swifter on doored buses.

It was evident that conductors, and therefore Routemasters, were being eclipsed by these developments. Many people could not stomach the final demise of the famous London icon, but there were others who couldn't wait to see them go. Tourist brochures often featured Routemasters and visitors to London wanted to see and ride on them. Many Londoners wanted to keep them, and it was often said that having a staff member readily available aided security. Others cited the help given by conductors to tourists and visitors. The reality, though, was often different. It soon became obvious to any regular passenger that, whilst most conductors still 'roamed' the vehicle and assisted passengers, some became little more than 'platform guards' and the appearance of a conductor upstairs became increasingly infrequent. Assaults on conductors were reported rather more often, and the comparison was soon made with 'bendy buses' where the driver had no cash on board. There were very few actual cash fares to be collected anyway, and it did seem that job satisfaction was suffering in the eyes of many conductors.

By the summer of 2002, even before all the refurbished RMs had been completed, thoughts were evidently turning to replacement of the last crew routes. Route 14 was the last crew route to be re-awarded (in April 2002) for continuing Routemaster operation with a start date in November 2002. It was widely believed that, although some routes might have to go, at least one such as the 14 would be safe until at least 2007. Some operators had fitted a few of their Routemasters with yet more new engines and gearboxes, with the intention of meeting new emissions regulations. In July 2002, though, Routemaster route 10 (Archway–Hammersmith) was announced for 'restructuring'; it was to be split, with

73
Newington Green
Islington Kings Cross
Euston Oxford Street
Hyde Park Corner

IAN BELL

the western end getting 'new buses', although failing to mention actual crew to driver only conversion. It duly came to pass that in February 2003 driver only buses converted the service. In December 2002 route 15 was re-awarded to Stagecoach through the normal five-year tendering process, but it was not mentioned at the time that it would convert to driver only buses. The same thing happened in February 2003 when route 11 was re-awarded to London General, as with the 15 for an unspecified start date later in 2003.

It was as though TfL and London Buses were fearful of making bold announcements of Routemaster conversions. However, new buses were soon ordered for the 15 and 11 and conversion dates were arranged in the autumn of 2003. Meanwhile, as other crew routes came round for re-tendering in the normal way, all were awarded for new driver only buses. As time passed, some routes came to be converted before their contract anniversary dates or without being re-tendered. These were often achieved after negotiations over the purchase of replacement buses, as operators were understandably loath to commit money to new bus purchases without the security of a reasonable ongoing contract period. Some other conversions were delayed beyond their anniversaries whilst waiting for new buses to arrive or, in the case of articulated buses on the 73 and then the 12, waiting for a suitable garage to be found.

However, all routes were converted by the end of 2005, leaving just a few RMs on TfL's 'heritage' routes. Others have been kept as special events vehicles by the operating companies, plus a large number in private preservation. The phenomenon of an RM or two (or even an RT type) turning out on the last or first day of a route change or operator change has quite taken off in recent times, and no doubt this will continue on suitable occasions. Indeed, since the withdrawals began in 2003, the vast majority of withdrawn Routemasters have been sold rather than scrapped. There will be many, many years yet where the odd Routemasters crop up at one-off operations and vehicle rallies. A full review follows, chronicling the countdown to the end.

COUNTDOWN TO THE END

Before recording the Routemaster run-down
that began in earnest in 2003, we should
record the fact that several Routemaster
routes received enhancements in the latter
half of 2002. They featured, along with
many other routes, in a whole series of
schemes across London in preparation for
what was expected to be a great increase in
passenger numbers once Congestion
Charging began in February 2003. Route 38
received more buses in July 2002 followed
by the 19 in August, the 6, 15 and 98 in
October, the 13 and 14 in November,
culminating in a slight enhancement on
route 159 from 4th January 2003.

To begin with, we present a route list as
at the beginning of 2003. Other than minor
adjustments and the more recent frequency
enhancements, the routes had lasted fairly
unscathed since the summer of 1992.
Indeed, in the intervening years, only
routes 3 and 2B (in 1993) and 139 (in 1998)
had been converted from crew operation,
leaving twenty routes at the turn of 2002/3,
with a total peak vehicle requirement (pvr)
by that stage of 565.

CAPITAL TRANSPORT

Route	Operator	Garage and pvr	Route terminals
6	Metroline	Willesden (pvr 28)	Willesden & Aldwych
7	First	Westbourne Park (pvr 13)	East Acton & Russell Square
8	Stagecoach	Bow (pvr 28)	Bow Church & Victoria
9	London United	Shepherd's Bush (pvr 17)	Hammersmith & Aldwych
10	Metroline	Holloway (pvr 24)	Hammersmith & Archway
11	London General	Stockwell (pvr 23)	Fulham Broadway & Liverpool Street
12	London Central	Camberwell (pvr 38)	Dulwich & Notting Hill Gate
13	Sovereign	Edgware (pvr 19)	Golders Green & Aldwych
14	London General	Putney (pvr 24)	Putney Heath & Tottenham Court Road
15	Stagecoach	Upton Park (pvr 26)	Paddington & Blackwall DLR (with journeys to East Ham)
19	Arriva	Battersea (pvr 26)	Finsbury Park & Battersea Bridge
22	London General	Putney (pvr 16)	Putney Common & Piccadilly Circus
23	First	Westbourne Park (pvr 30)	Westbourne Park & Liverpool Street
36	London Central	New Cross (pvr 47)	Lewisham & Queen's Park
38	Arriva	Clapton (pvr 50)	Clapton Pond & Victoria
73	Arriva	Tottenham (pvr 55)	Tottenham & Victoria
94	London United	Shepherd's Bush (pvr 21)	Acton Green & Piccadilly Circus
98	Metroline	Willesden (pvr 25)	Willesden & Holborn
137	Arriva	Brixton (pvr 27)	Streatham Hill & Oxford Circus
159	Arriva	Brixton (pvr 28)	Streatham (old garage) & Marble Arch

2003

The first major change of 2003 came on 1st February, when Routemaster routes 7, 9, 94 and 137 continued the process from 2002. All four received additional buses, with pvr increases of +7, +4, +3 and +2 respectively. However, route 10 was re-structured and the replacement for its northern end, route 390, had just 17 buses instead of the 24 that had been on the 10. And so the total pvr reached 574, the highest in recent times, and a figure which was to last just one week. In any case, the pvrs on several Routemaster routes still had to be partly made up of doored buses anyway, albeit in crew mode, so the numbers of buses needed were never made up by the presence of actual RMs.

CAPITAL TRANSPORT

Back to the 10, though, and it was a rather confused and complicated business all round. In a set of major proposals for enhancements in central London issued by TfL in April 2002, a particular need was to increase the number of buses overall between Knightsbridge and Hammersmith. Historically, the 10 – itself a spin-off from a split of the 73 some years before – only ran from the west as far as King's Cross, with just garage and positioning journeys running on to the garage. In more recent times, though, a full service had been created along York Way. The route was based at Holloway Garage, but the running time needed to get right through to Hammersmith and back within crew duty times was causing many Number 10s to be curtailed. Short turns at Hyde Park Corner and Kensington Olympia were becoming very frequent, putting even greater pressure on route 9.

The proposal was to keep the 10 number on the main Hammersmith to King's Cross section, and to create a generous overlap by adding a new route 390 from Marble Arch to Archway. In May 2002, the revised 10 was offered to tender and within just two months was awarded to First with new driver only buses. The confusion, though, was that this section was listed as the 390. The Marble Arch – Archway service was to stay as the 10 with Metroline on a 'modified existing contract' basis for about 20 months, until due for re-tender in its own right. In the event, the route numbers were changed back to the original proposals and from 1st February 2003 the Marble Arch – Archway route kept its Routemasters, but now as the 390. It was never an especially busy service compared with the new 10, and it was often thought that it had been really intended that the Hammersmith end would keep the RMs rather than the northern section. Eight former London General TfL-owned RMLs moved to Willesden, here to replace some Metrobuses in use as crew buses on routes 6 and 98. It introduced Iveco engined RMLs to what had been a Cummins garage.

The next change came from 8th February 2003 when the 36 was 'restructured' in a partial driver-only conversion. The April 2002 proposals had identified the busy route 36 corridor as needing more capacity. The solution here was to retain Routemasters on route 36 between Queen's Park and New Cross, but with about half of its frequency taken over as new route 436 between Paddington and Lewisham, using articulated single-deck buses. On 8th February the 36 had its pvr reduced from 47 to 26 Routemasters, whilst the 436 gained 26 Citaros. Several of the RMs released from route 36 moved over to Putney for an enhancement on the 22, others went to Camberwell to assist the existing allocation on route 12 and to Stockwell for similar use on the 11. Five of the 'Marshall' RMs were returned to TfL and were immediately re-issued to First at Westbourne Park, here to

reduce the number of Metrobuses on the 7 and 23. Eleven RMLs were acquired by TfL and distributed to Arriva, London United and Metroline, in each case to replace doored buses on crew routes.

London General's route 22 was the last Routemaster route to receive an enhancement before the Central London Congestion Charging scheme began on 17th February. Intended for three more buses from 8th February, the change was deferred one week to 15th. The total pvr over the whole Routemaster fleet had now reached 556, and no further changes to totals of any consequence took place in the ensuing three years of the gradual conversion programme.

RML 2295 Kensington
RM 2128 Edgware Road

Routine tender offers of Routemaster routes continued and, as with the announcement of the 15 on 4th December 2002, then the 11 in February 2003, the 23 in March and the 94 in April the awards all failed to actually mention words such as 'driver only'. Phrases such as 'further information to be given later' were written. By April, it became known that the 11 and 23 would be 'converted during the life of the contract'. In any case new buses had already been ordered for the 15, followed very soon for those for the 11 and 23. By the time that the 6 and 98 were announced on 6th June, though, it did admit that driver only buses would be introduced, and this became the norm. Actual start dates often varied from nominal contract dates, in the event, but that was often to suit vehicle availability. All contract awards through to the end of Routemaster operation were to the incumbent operator.

In March, Sovereign London's TfL-owned RMs on route 13 gained proper RM fleet numbers after having had purely numerical numbers allocated by Sovereign. Arriva's gold liveried RM 6, painted thus for H.M. The Queen's Golden Jubilee in 2002, stayed in gold throughout 2003, and indeed was still in that condition and used only for special events through to 2005. On the night of 29/30th March, Metroline's RMs and RMLs on route 390 moved from Holloway Garage to a new site on York Way at King's Cross. Perhaps if that move had been possible a year earlier, it would not have been necessary for the old 10 to be split. In May 2003, the first of six RMs being refurbished by Arriva – Marshall Bus having closed down by this time – went into service at Battersea. It was RM 1292, and would eventually be followed by RMs 54, 85, 346, 713 and 1975, although it took until March 2004 for this small programme to be completed. These were destined to have a very short second service life.

On 22nd April, Stagecoach's RML 2272 suffered an accident whilst on route 15. At first thought to be a write-off, it was sold to Sullivan Buses and subsequently returned to service; it was the first direct RML sale from a London company for many years. Most, but not all, accidents affecting other RMLs over the next couple of years tended

to result in the buses being withdrawn for disposal, rather than them being repaired. Sullivan's RML 2272 later appeared on all sorts of special services in later months and years, including for Armchair on the Kingston park and ride K50 service on 20th December 2003.

Although the part conversions of the 10 and 36 earlier in the year were not marked in any special way, all that was to change with the 15, which had been set for 30th August. Stagecoach staged a special event on the previous Bank Holiday weekend 24/25th August when RM 980 and Green Line liveried RMC 1461 worked special journeys on east London routes 101, 104, 115, 147, 238 and 330. On the last crew day itself Friday 29th August, red RMC 1456, green RMC 1461, standard RM 980, RML 2456 newly painted in old LT green country area livery as a 'last day surprise', plus AEC-engined RML 2760 all supported the decreasing numbers of normal RMLs on the 15. They were supported by guest vehicles all contributed by other owners and operators. This set the pattern for future 'last days' and a whole range of 'guest vehicles' in various degrees appeared at most subsequent conversions. RML 2760 was the last bus into Upton Park Garage, its bonnet draped in a Union flag. Five Routemasters passed to private owners, including RMC 1461 to Cobham Bus Museum, half-a-dozen moved over to Bow for continuing use on route 8, whilst the majority of redundant buses went immediately to dealer Ensign Bus for re-sale.

Another minor change from 30th August was the conversion of the late evening and Sunday services on route 94 back from crew to driver-only operation, now that more one-person buses were at Shepherd's Bush Garage. Then from 1st November 2003 it was the turn of the Monday to Friday service on route 11, the conversion having been deferred from the formal date of 28th June. Already, Routemasters did not work on Saturdays or Sundays. London General's Commercial Services' RM 9 and DRM 2516 were loaned to the operational fleet to work the last crew journeys. Stockwell's RMs and RMLs were moved for continuing use to Putney (routes 14 and 22) and Camberwell (12).

RML 2610 Regent Street
RML 2669 Buckingham
Palace Road

GERALD MEAD

RML 2740 Queen Victoria Street
RMLs 2555, 2724 and 2553 Oxford Street
RM 871 Aldwych

CAPITAL TRANSPORT

CAPITAL TRANSPORT

First's route 23 was converted from 15th November, the contract renewal having been deferred since 23rd August. The last crew journey on the previous evening was with RML 885, driven by Leon Daniels, First's Divisional Director London & SE and conducted by Peter Hendy, M.D. of Surface Transport TfL. Eight of the RMLs were sent to First in Glasgow, where one or two were eventually used on sightseeing tours and private hire work there; some later moved on to other First subsidiaries. Seven of the eight 'Marshall' RMs from First passed via TfL to Arriva, who topped up their allocations on routes 19 and 38 with them. Interestingly, some of these retained their yellow relief bands from First days into Arriva operation. RM 1650 was kept back by First, and in early 2004 was repainted to silver, recalling the bus of that number that had been in that livery in 1977 for H.M. The Queen's Silver Jubilee. It was unveiled in Silver Jubilee colours at Paddington on 1st April 2004 displaying fleet number SRM 3. Other RMLs released by the route 23 conversion languished for a while in store, but were eventually sold off over a lengthy period.

Routemasters After Dark

Philip Wallis

Philip Wallis has made a speciality of photographing buses at work late at night. The next few pages show some of his work with Routemasters between 2003 and December 2005.

RML 2372 Tottenham Court Road
RML 2570 Piccadilly
RML 2612 Piccadilly

RML 2304 New Oxford Street
RM 1119 Victoria
RM 2071 Baker Street
RML 2382 Cambridge Circus

RML 2302 Notting Hill Gate
RML 2275 Notting Hill Gate
RML 2367 Tottenham Court Road

RM 541 Victoria
RM 1980 Queens Park
RM 2122 Charing Cross Road
RML 2491 Whitehall
RML 2567 Piccadilly
RML 2730 Haymarket

2004

The first conversion of 2004 came on 24th January, when the weekday service on London United's route 94 succumbed. In this case, the original contract renewal date of 18th October 2003 had taken effect, but the type conversion had to wait until 24th January 2004 once vehicles had been delivered. Even so, many entered service in crew mode as early as possible. The last crew bus was RML 2500, duplicated by the traditional liveried RML 880. The first RMLs taken off service were the five TfL owned machines that had been transferred in when the 36 had been converted one year earlier, but they were put into so-called 'warm storage' at Tolworth Garage until eventually sold in the autumn of 2004. Several of the RMLs released from the 94 were still needed for the 9 for another seven months, as they enabled the removal of seven Metrobuses that had been in use as crew buses. Otherwise, most of the rest were sold to Mike Nash of Cobham for re-sale.

Metroline's routes 6 and 98 were next for conversion, from 27th March. As happened on the 94, the original contract renewal date on 13th December 2003 had been implemented. Again, the replacement buses started to appear in crew mode in the weeks before the type conversion date. Although the last crew journeys were with standard Willesden-based RMLs, 2431 on the 6 and 2430 on the 98, the company's own 'heritage vehicles' Metrobus M 1 and RMC 1513 also worked on the last crew day. Eleven of Willesden's large RML fleet moved over to King's Cross to replace withdrawn sisters there, another eleven went to Blue Triangle for storage, spares or re-sale, but the majority were sold to private owners. A few passed on to other London area operators Timebus Travel at South Mimms and International Coaches at Thornton Heath. In each case, some of these were soon overhauled and repainted, soon re-appearing as private hire vehicles around London.

An interesting disposal in March 2004 was of RML 2317. It passed from London General to fellow Go-Ahead company Metrobus. Soon it was repainted to country area green and it appeared later in the year at some special events and as a 'guest vehicle' on later Routemaster route conversions. RMLs 2725 and 2732 in the Commercial Services fleet gained cream relief bands, and 2725 had General fleetnames. These, together with RM 9, were kept in pristine condition and often appeared on London General's summer special services, for example on the occasions of the Epsom Derby and Wimbledon Tennis.

RML 880 Oxford Circus
RM 848 Piccadilly Circus

Over
RML 902 Queens Park
RML 2537 Oxford Street
RML 2431 Lower Regent St

23

At Stagecoach, RML 2760, which had suffered a series of engine problems, went back into service on 15th March on route 8 and stayed in use thereon until the last crew day of that service. It was joined by Stagecoach's other 'special' the green liveried RML 2456 and both made fine sights in the West End on daily service. The contract renewal date for route 8 was maintained as 26th June, but the driver-only type conversion was brought forward to 5th June. As had happened in 2003, on the preceding Bank Holiday weekend 30th/31st May Stagecoach arranged an ambitious 'running day' using RMLs 2456 and 2760 on a whole range of fourteen routes, seven past and seven current, all over east London. By the last crew day of route 8 on Friday 4th June, at least half the scheduled service was being worked by Tridents. A very large con-

tingent of guest vehicles ran extra journeys. A few were Stagecoach's own specials, including RML 2665 newly outshopped in national Stagecoach colours. The Museum's prototype Routemaster RM 1 came out in service, thus allowing the first and last Routemaster (2760) to be in use together on the same route for the first time. RML 2760 was the last in service and, like when it was used on the 15 in 2003, it had a Union flag over its bonnet. A few withdrawn RMLs were sold privately, but the majority went into storage at Stagecoach depots at Chesterfield, Carlisle and Preston. The intention was to keep them for any eventuality, which had not materialised even one year later. Six of them suffered in the floods at Carlisle on 8th January 2005 and had to be nominally written off. Even so, they did get sold on to Ensign Bus for potential re-use.

RMLs 2429, 2450
New Oxford Street

CAPITAL TRANSPORT

CAPITAL TRANSPORT

CAPITAL TRANSPORT

KIM RENNIE

RML 2607 Oxford Street
RML 2760 Bow

27

CAPITAL TRANSPORT

First became the next operator to lose its last Routemaster route, the 7. This route had been renewed from 24th June 2000 with a seven year contract but it was always intended that a crew-to-opo conversion would take place during the life of the contract at an unspecified date. This duly occurred from 3rd July 2004, using Tridents made spare elsewhere, from the loss of route 25 to Stagecoach East London. On Sunday 20th June, silver RM 1650 (SRM 3) and RML 2735 were both used on route 25

to mark the last operation of that service by First. By the last crew day of the 7, both RMLs 885 and 2735 had received cream relief bands and gold London Transport fleetnames, and the last crew journey on the 7 was duly performed by RML 885. As had become the norm, several guest vehicles joined in. Withdrawn RMLs were parked at a yard near White City, and eventually most were sold to Ensign Bus. RML 2735 and RM 1650, together with open-top Routemasters RM 120 and RMC 1510 were retained by First as a 'heritage fleet', and can be used at special events for the company.

Arriva's route 137 followed one week later. The contract did not get renewed until 18th September but the conversion from crew operation was brought forward to 10th July. New buses had already arrived and they were put into use as soon as possible and indeed by the last crew day just five Routemasters were left in operation. Enthusiastic staff at Brixton Garage ensured that the last journeys were worked by the type, and RML 2407 performed the last crew journey. In this instance, it was RMLs that continued on the 159 and about two dozen RMs passed to Ensign, even though some had recently been re-engined.

Two of Arriva's buses were treated to special liveries as part of the 'RM 50' celebrations later in July. RM 25 was brown and yellow whilst RML 2524 was green, the former entering service on route 19 on 23rd July, the latter on the next morning, and both stayed thereon until the spring of 2005. TfL-owned RML 2360 was fitted out for the Design Exhibition at Earl's Court in September, and was painted externally in Arriva livery. Arriva's RM 275 was decked out as a mock 'triple-decker' to promote a Harry Potter film, and later in the year was replaced by RM 2217 in a similar garb, the latter lasting in this guise until June 2005. Building up to the last crew days of route 73, Arriva's RM 5, still fitted with an AEC engine, was used, along with RTW 467, on special journeys on Tottenham Garage routes 41, 76 and 243 on 2nd September. Subsequently, Arriva have retained RM 5 and 2217, as well as gold RM 6, in their fleet for occasional private hire or future special use.

CAPITAL TRANSPORT

RML 2498 Paddington
RM 275 North Weald

29

RM 1312 Oxford Circus
RML 2559 Bishops Bridge Rd

RML 2674 Battersea
RML 2692 Knightsbridge
RM 2217 Oxford Street
RM 1398 Clapham Common

CAPITAL TRANSPORT

KEVIN SMITH

MARK KEHOE

The Routemaster 50 Event   Andrew Morgan

RM 1 followed by RML 3 passes some of the other Routemaster 50 entrants.

Right from when planning started 2½ years before the event, and when London RM operations were actually still on the increase, Routemaster 50 was to be a commemoration of RM 1 being 50 years old and a celebration of the type; at no point was this event intended to be a goodbye to London Routemaster service or to commemorate the end of London Routemaster operations. Many people, however, from the ranks of enthusiasts and the media at large, seized upon this event to publicise the demise of the Routemaster and lend support to a Save the Routemaster campaign.

In late 2001 plans commenced and a Routemaster 50 Committee was established to organise the event. Colin Curtis, former chief engineer of London Buses, Honorary President of the Routemaster Association and one of the survivors of the Routemaster design team, volunteered to chair the Committee. The first priority was to look for a suitable venue and initial attention was paid to the Royal Parks with the perhaps ambitious idea of using Hyde Park. It was quickly obvious that there were far too many obstacles in the way for this site to be used and our attentions were re-focused on numerous other parks around London.

34

In late 2001 and early 2002, an approach was made to the London Borough of Wandsworth for Battersea Park, but it was obvious that this local authority could not look this far in advance. This caused a serious delay in the organisation of the event and when they did respond they quoted a horrifyingly high price for the hire of the park for the weekend. With requirements such as the size of the park, hard standing, access and location amongst some very specific conditions, we quickly narrowed down the list of possible alternatives. Finsbury Park had been used in the 1990s by the RT/RF Register and therefore was a known possibility and early discussions with the London Borough of Haringey were encouraging on all issues. So in January 2003, the venue was settled as Finsbury Park and the advance publicity commenced to make sure that the date was booked in everyone's diary before anybody else had any better ideas.

Colin Curtis then assembled a team to organise various aspects of the event. With his experience some twenty years previously at the Chiswick Works open days, he was able to recruit names from outside the Routemaster Association. Examples of these included the Friends of London's Transport Museum, the London Bus Preservation Trust and many others who had been involved with London's transport over the years of the Routemaster.

For the site itself, toilets had to be hired, skips ordered, first aid cover sourced, advertising and publicity arranged and booked, bus blinds and timetables organised and agreed for a special bus route, X50, arrangements for vehicle movements with the Metropolitan Police and local bus companies, site signage ordered and sourced, marshalls recruited to assist with the vehicle movements over the weekend, sales stand bookings, public liability insurance arranged, a dedicated website set up and maintained, vehicle entries collated and information sent out to the owners, and the list just went on endlessly.

Large round vinyls with the Routemaster 50 logo in gold were manufactured and supplied by the Routemaster Association to the London operators, although in the end they were only applied immediately before the event. The first to appear were on route 73 from 17th July. Routes 12, 14, 22, 36 (London Central/General) and 19, 73 (Arriva) were known to participate. The original idea was for them to be applied to the nearside lower panels below the lower deck windows although Arriva at Tottenham garage applied them immediately in front of the advert panels. Naturally, permission to apply these logos had to be obtained from TfL and most stayed on the vehicles until the end of the year when the operating companies finally reacted to an edict from TfL for them to be removed. Due to the

RM 470, from Germany where it is used on promotional work, and SRM 3, which ran special journeys over the event weekend.

MARK KEHOE

ER 880 with the Routemaster 50 logo, launched to coincide with the Routemaster 50 rally.

existing route branding, Arriva's Clapton garage was unable to apply them to most of their RMLs and therefore route 38 did not feature these logos at all. This then produced a surplus of vinyls that then found themselves on to various preserved vehicles and also on London United's ER 880 and Stagecoach's RML 2665.

An event of this scale would normally require substantial sponsorship, but despite a concerted effort to find suitable (or willing) sponsors, no major contributors were found. The Routemaster Association therefore took the risk that if the event was to fail due to weather or any unforeseen incident (such as terrorist action), all costs for the event would have to be covered by them. Various ways at trying to recover these costs were looked into. It was impossible to levy an admission charge to a public venue such as Finsbury Park (and

probably impractical to implement as well) and therefore all revenue had to be raised through sales of stalls or merchandise on the day. A limited range of souvenir merchandise to commemorate the anniversary was commissioned by the Association and generally these sold very quickly and very well. The biggest single source of income was from programme sales. These had to be priced quite high but as there was no admission charge we hoped that potential purchasers would not be put off. In the end the event cost the Association nearly £30,000 to organise and stage; luckily the weather was kind and enthusiasts and the general public at large supported the event in their thousands. Numerous people, organisations, and companies all helped in various ways, and without all this generous help, this event would not have been possible.

No event would be complete without buses operating some form of service. It was not possible to have the number of moving vehicles that carried passengers at Routemaster 40, but with the help of Arriva London, and the agreement of TfL, a free bus service numbered X50 operated from Manor House station to Tottenham and Stamford Hill. It ran two-thirds full during most of both days with a number of different vehicles, including many notable examples. On the Saturday the vehicles used were: London's Transport Museum's RM 1, Cobham Bus Museum's RML 3, Arriva's RM 6, London Central's RM 9, Blue Triangle's RM 298, Philip Groves's RM 809 (from Sweden), Ian Hoskin's RM 938, Sovereign London's Euro 3 engined RM 1562, First's RMC 1510 and SRM 3 (RM 1650), Stagecoach London's RML 2456 and RML 2760, Shaftesbury & District's RME 1 (the lengthened RMA 29), and, as an extra, London's Transport Museum's FRM 1. On the Sunday the vehicles were: Blue Triangle's RM 298 and RML 900, Philip Groves's RM 809, Green Lane's RMC 1469, Sovereign London's RM 1562, Past Times Buses' RM 1859, Arriva's RM 2217, Shaftesbury & District's RME 1, and, again as an extra, London's Transport Museum's FRM 1.

One should not forget route 19, which operated with Routemasters as normal all weekend to its adjacent terminus at Finsbury Park station, and also with two special liveried vehicles (Great Northern RM 25 and Shillibeer liveried RML 2524) that officially started in passenger service on the first day of the event. And if this was not enough, First London operated Routemasters throughout the weekend on various journeys on route 259, which passed Finsbury Park, using open top RMC 1510, silver jubilee liveried RM 1650 (SRM 3), and RML 2735.

We had hoped that this event would exceed the achievements of the Routemaster 40 event from 1994 in several ways; we had hoped that there would be in excess of 100 Routemasters involved in the event – there were 96 involved with Routemaster 40 – and it was generally believed that this would probably be the last occasion that it would be possible to organise an event to commemorate Routemasters in London. Over the two days there were 98 Routemasters with almost every variant possible exhibited. In total there were fifty-eight RMs, twelve RMCs, five RCLs, twenty RMLs, one RMA, one RMF, and one FRM. Notable too was the number of privately owned, and newly acquired, RMLs at the event, making this the largest ever gathering of Routemasters at one special event (and possibly the largest ever gathering of one type of bus that has ever been organised).

In hindsight it was probably not surprising, but at the time the location of the event at Finsbury Park was getting some criticism from vehicle owners and potential takers of sales stands. It is known that some vehicles stayed away because of concerns of security on site. To say that there were some interesting characters in the park would be an understatement. In the end, it was commented by many visitors that the atmosphere of the event was excellent and there was no reported trouble. It will never be known how many visitors attended the event; it was unique in that there was no admission charge and that any passer-by, any local resident or park user, or any member of the general public could be present. The friendly atmosphere extended to many industry professionals, vehicle owners and enthusiasts that were re-united for the first time in many years.

Despite the ever-rising fuel costs, vehicles did come long distances to the event. Notable ones for a furthest travelled award included RMC 1485 from Edinburgh (the Mac Tours' fleet), RM 7 from Yorkshire, RM 1101 from Birkenhead, RM 1414 from Manchester, RML 2701 from Wigan, RM 912 and RMC 1469 from the Isle of Wight. From outside the UK came RM 470 from Germany and RM 809 from Sweden. We also had Routemaster Association members from Canada, Bermuda and all across Europe in attendance. A BBC television film crew followed RM 809 and RM 912 to the event and a feature was screened on the BBC London regional *Inside Out* programme on 27th September. RM 912 had been completely rebuilt from a cannibalised wreck and returned to roadworthy condition for the event.

The line-up of RM 1, RML 3, RMC 4 and RMs 5–10.

One memory from this event is the much talked about line up of Routemasters along the southern internal roadway that just seemed to go on forever: precision parking would be an understatement. It was even noted that this line-up had a no-man's area in front of the vehicles for the benefit of the dozens of photographers present.

As you walked down the line of Routemasters, it was quickly obvious that every vehicle had a unique story to tell; some had operated for several owners, some had been re-engined twice, some had been restored over a long period, some were now promotional vehicles, some were now back as a bus again after another use, some had been repainted for this event, some were being rallied for the first time after a long absence, and the list continues.

On the Saturday, Cobham's RM 3 drove into the site with its lower front panels covered over in white paper and then became the star as it was unveiled at one o'clock with its new front grille. "New" is probably the wrong description, but RM 3 had been rebuilt with a replica of its original radiator grille, bonnet and wings. Naturally it had been re-numbered back to RML 3, and has become the first of the prototypes to be restored to original condition.

On the Sunday, Mick Biddell's RMF 1254 became the star of the show. RMF 1254 was last rallied after it had been acquired from Northern General in 1980; now, twenty four years later it has been fully restored to original 1962 London condition and the standard of restoration especially after it had been seen standing around for so long unloved, was truly breathtaking.

Many RMs returned to London for the first time in many years specially for the event. A vehicle of particular note was the appearance of RM 7. This was the first time that RM 7 had ever been at a rally since its Yorkshire based owner acquired it from London Buses in 1986. It had been tested and licensed the week before the event and appeared in as-withdrawn condition. Museum exhibits making a rare return to London included RM 506 which was newly restored from the Aston Manor Museum in Birmingham, RM 1101 in purple and gold Golden Jubilee livery from the Wirral Transport Museum at Birkenhead and RM 1414 from the Greater Manchester Museum. London's Transport Museum RM 2 remained under restoration and therefore the decision was made not to bring it to the event, but nevertheless the unique line-up of RMs 1, 3–10 was achieved.

On the Sunday there were the two processions. The morning procession was a parade of the important London Transport bus types. The vehicles were K 424, T 31,

T 219, STL 2377, RT 2177, RTL 139, RTW 29 and RF 366 along with RM 1, RML 2760 and FRM 1. Various owners including the London's Transport Museum and the London Bus Preservation Trust provided these as guest vehicles. On the Sunday afternoon, the parade was of Routemaster types with RM 1, RML 3, RMC 4, RM 5, gold liveried RM 6, RM 7, RM 8, RM 254, RME 1, Harry Potter liveried RM 275, open top RMC 1510, Green Line liveried RCL 2229, RM 470, RML 2760 and FRM 1.

Other vehicles in attendance on the site were a Bussing D2U 64 registered B-ZU-629H from Berlin in Germany, Metrobus M 1349 which was used for a turn-over demonstration by Queens Motors (which demonstrated the recovery of an overturned bus by the use of airbags), DML 17 from London Central which was used for the bus pull on the Saturday, PDL 16 and 18 from Arriva which were used for advert posting for children, hospitality bus DW 93 from Arriva, and a Leyland National mobile shop GAU728L.

The Lady Mayor of Haringey was due to visit at 2pm on the Saturday afternoon but she arrived early and started her own tour. We suspected that the event would attract some television and press coverage, but we had not been prepared for the numbers that were present over the weekend as media

interest in the event was far and wide. Whether it was the scale of the event that was so visible to the public, or the publicity that the Routemaster in London was getting at the time due to the on-going withdrawal programme, is open to debate. As well as newspaper journalists and photographers, we had television crews from the United Kingdom, Sky News (who broadcast live from the site), German, Middle Eastern, Australian, and Chinese crews just to mention a few. This number of television crews present was previously an unheard of feature of a bus rally. Numerous newspaper articles were located on the event, including The Guiyang Daily (from the Guizhou province in the south west of China), Daily Times in Pakistan, and The Strait Times in Singapore. Also in Australia, the Bus and Truck Museum at Tempe were celebrating Routemaster 50 with their RM (1708) giving rides around the streets of Sydney.

It has long been a feature of RMOOA events that a good quality rally plaque was produced for the event and this event was no exception. Each vehicle entry that arrived over the weekend was presented with a brass rally plaque. It was an exhausting weekend for the organisers – but thoroughly rewarding, enjoyable and one of those events that may never be repeated or surpassed.

RM 25 and RML 2524 were painted in special liveries just before the Routemaster 50 rally and entered service on the 19 on the Saturday. RM 25 is seen at Finsbury Park and RML 2524 at Battersea.

2004

Saturday 4th September was the biggest conversion day yet, with three routes and around 100 Routemasters replaced. It was also the most controversial as the 73 was the first crew route to be fully and directly converted to articulated single-deck buses. Because of the larger capacity now provided, albeit at the expense of many seats, there was a heavy pvr reduction from 55 to just 41 (later increased to 43). The contract renewal date for the 73 had been deferred from 1st May to 4th September because of the difficulty in finding a suitable operating base for the new vehicles, and even then this was only resolved at the last minute. There were also alleged problems at certain points along the route but this proved to be unfounded. Because the route was being converted to a new style of vehicle, for the first time in the series of conversions the 73 retained its full allocation of Routemasters right until the last day. RM 5 performed the last crew working on the 73, bringing to an end 42 years of continuous Routemaster operation on the route. A considerable number of RMLs were parked up at Tottenham Marshes storage depot after the conversion, those owned by Arriva passing to Ensign Bus. However, those that had been owned by TfL and leased to Arriva remained in store until February 2005, after which they were then swiftly sold off to dealers and private owners.

London United and Metroline ceased Routemaster operation when routes 9 and 390 were converted from 4th September, both contracts being renewed on the correct due day. Route 9 saw many new vehicles take over prior to the official conversion date, such that only four Routemasters were actually running by the last day. Although there were a few guest vehicle workings on the last crew day, several others performed two days earlier on Wednesday 1st. RML 880 was of course in the forefront of all this, and duly ran the last crew journey. Other than a couple of RMLs that were allocated to London Sovereign to assist on route 13, and the retention of RML 880 as a special events vehicle, the rest of LU's RMLs were sold off in ones and twos to private owners and dealers over the next few months. A notable disposal was of five RMLs for tours.

A particularly notable occurrence was on Saturday 28th August when special dispensation was given to operate RM 2033 and RML 880 on the 9 over Hammersmith Bridge, albeit with restricted passenger loadings. The bridge had been subject to a weight restriction for twelve years and otherwise only Darts operated across it in passenger service. There were several round trips through to the traditional terminus of the 9 to the site of the former Mortlake Garage. On 29th and 30th August, a few RMs and RMLs returned to the 94 for just those two days, working extras on the occasion of the Notting Hill Carnival. The Carnival also featured the last appearance of Routemasters from London Central on the special 12X and 36X services from south London. This had been a feature of Carnival for several years.

At Metroline, the 390 became the shortest lived Routemaster number of recent times, and again new buses were delivered in plenty of time and replaced many of the Routemasters as they were made ready for service. RML 2731 was the last crew bus in to King's Cross, and several guest vehicles ran on the last day. Indeed, some of these were operated through to Hammersmith as 10s, recalling the recent past before the route was split and supporting the extra buses on the 9 on that section. Other than RML 903, which had been a 'special' vehicle at Holloway Garage for several years, the remaining Routemasters were soon sold off.

RML 903 itself made a one-day return to the 390 on 19th November when it ran some journeys with fares collected going to the BBC's Children in Need Appeal. It had also run back on 26th June on route 17 on the occasion of Holloway Garage's open day. Another example was with London General, this time with a special one-off operation on a route that had not seen a Routemaster for nearly 34 years. RML 2535 operated several journeys between Putney and Kingston on route 85 on 4th December, in aid of the Christmas Appeals of the Mayors of the two Boroughs at each end of the route. Indeed, it had become commonplace by this time for 'guest vehicles' on the various routes to collect fares and donations which, with TfL's approval, would go to a nominated charity.

RML 2660 King's Cross
RM 5 Oxford Street

Fall in number of seats as bendy buses take over

By Ross Lydall
Local Government Correspondent

THOUSANDS of commuters on London's busiest bus route are to be forced to stand.

Transport for London is to nearly halve the number of seats on route 73 when bendy buses take over from Routemasters.

A total of 55 Routemasters, which run between Victoria and Tottenham, will be replaced by 41 bendies next month — cutting the number of seats from 3,960 to

Thousands will have to stand for journeys

2,009. Rush-hour frequencies on the only route to cover the entire length of Oxford Street will also be reduced when the £200,000 bendy buses are introduced next month.

Hundreds of passengers have signed a petition calling for the 73

route to keep its Routemasters, claiming they will be forced to travel miles without a seat.

And Oxford Street businesses have expressed alarm — warning that the already-congested road will come to a halt as the new 18-metre buses queue at stops.

CAPITAL TRANSPORT

42

esreview

It's not only Londoners who have been outraged by the Mayor's decision to abandon the beloved Routemaster ...

BY ANDREW GILLIGAN

International favourite: foreign news coverage (inset) reminds us that the Routemaster is admired as much abroad as at home

The world asks why scrap this bus?

SOMETIMES in this country, it takes outsiders to show us the full measure of what we're losing. It is not just the people of London, in their thousands, who have objected to Ken Livingstone's plan to abolish the Routemaster. Unlike almost any other specifically London story before it, this one is also winning the attention, and the disbelief, of the world.

It's full-page news in the Philadelphia Inquirer ("Riders Fight Plan To Idle London Buses"). Holland's Goudsche Courant is in mourning for "*de rode icoon*". CNN and the Washington Post have covered the Evening Standard's campaign. Even NBC's mighty Today show, breakfast fodder of Middle America, awarded the Routemaster a precious "segment", calling it "a classic slice of London life lost". From the Melbourne Herald-Sun to the Singapore Straits Times, France's La Croix to the Frankfurter Rundschau, the Johannesburg Sunday Times to the Rocky Mountain News, the world has been reading and writing about the premature execution of an old red bus. And the question the world has been asking is: "Why?"

The Baltimore Sun condemned the replacement buses as having "the manoeuvrability of rolling buildings" and found an 84-year-old, partially disabled Routemaster user who poohpoohed Transport for London's claim that the bus was unsuitable for the likes of him. The San Francisco Chronicle made unflattering comparisons between London's transport heritage-phobia and its own city's decision to preserve vintage cable-cars and trams.

The scale of international interest — with more than 70 foreign media outlets covering the story to date — is perhaps not surprising. For decades, the Routemaster has not merely transported Londoners from Trafalgar Square to Peckham. With equal efficiency, it has also transported everyone else to London from any TV or cinema screen on earth. In an age when nations are encouraged to put an economic value on national symbols, it is a valuable part of Britain's brand.

The Routemaster appears on the cover of no fewer than six of the 12 main London tourist guides, including the Time Out guide, the Amazon UK bestseller. It must be doubtful whether any future guidebook designer will ever bother getting that exciting bendy bus snap out of the picture library. Type "Routemaster" into the Google search engine and the third most popular result is a fan club in, of all places, Luxembourg, proud owners of an original bus. The 11th most popular is the website of the Netherlands Routemaster Association, dedicated to the "ultimate form of English public transport", the Routemaster "*dubbeldekkerbus*".

But it's not just the Dutch to whom the buses say London. Mary Nicholson, in High Street Kensington from Christchurch, New Zealand, and hoping to get to Piccadilly Circus, was sorry to hear that the last Routemaster route to do the journey, the No 9, had been axed the week before. It has been replaced by a type of modern double-decker, outstandingly charmless even by the standards of the breed, that looks like a large red microwave oven.

"The old buses are part of London and they're part of what we came to London to see," said Ms Nicholson, heading for the Tube station. "For you to get rid of them when you don't need to — it's self-mutilation, really. It's like cutting off a part of your own body."

And as for the Mayor's proposed "heritage" route — likely to run between a few central London tourist attractions during daylight hours only — neither visitors nor Londoners seem particularly interested. "Nobody wants a sort of Disney route that isn't part of the proper network and will probably only last a few years," said Ben Brook, of the Save the Routemaster campaign. "That isn't saving the Routemaster as far as we are concerned."

THE Routemaster may be a global symbol of London, but the trouble is that for the Mayor, it seems to be the wrong symbol. Routemaster campaigners have long been mystified about the real reasons why Mr Livingstone turned from an ardent supporter of the buses less than two years ago into their present-day nemesis. Certainly, none of the arguments TfL puts forward, about the safety record of the open-rear platform, disabled access and so on, is in any way new or has in any way changed since 2002. Many are convinced that the Mayor has decided that the old buses are simply not fashionable, incompatible with the shiny, modern image he seeks to project for the capital. Pubs, Routemasters and churches out; skyscrapers, gazpacho and the London Eye in.

If this is the reason, it is wrong on two levels. First, it is not a true reflection of the city. London is no more simply modern than it is simply historic; just like the bus fleet, it is a mixture of both. More fundamentally, the Routemaster transcends fashion. "It is a classic," says Brook. "It will still look right on the streets in 10 years' time, whereas the bendy buses will date badly, long before that." One of the reasons London remains so attractive to visitors, despite its terrible weather and ridiculous prices, is that it is unique. With the demise of the Routemaster, part of that uniqueness will be ripped away.

● Sign the internet petition at www.petitiononline.com/routemas/petition
● Tell your friends and work colleagues about the petition and get them to sign too.
● Write to Ken Livingstone, Mayor of London, at City Hall, London SE1 2AA, email him at mayor@london.gov.uk, or phone the Mayor's Public Liaison Line on 020 7983 4100 to tell him your views. (Politely).
● Tell us if you have any interesting news or information about the Routemaster on routemaster@standard.co.uk. Confidentiality assured.

RML 2731 King's Cross
RML 2389 York Way
RML 2731 Torriano Avenue

46

RML 2447 Piccadilly
RM 848 Olympia
RML 2463 Kensington

The last conversion of 2004 was of route 12 from 6th November and it was the second complete conversion to articulated buses. Like the 73, the route suffered a pvr reduction, this time from 38 to 29 buses. Once again, problems with getting a suitable base and sorting out the terminal arrangements at both ends of the route at Dulwich and Oxford Circus caused the contract renewal to be deferred from 31st July to 6th November. Accommodation at Camberwell Garage was available, but only after the loss of some routes elsewhere to another operator a month earlier, and by subsequent re-allocation of other routes. The 12 was cut back from Notting Hill Gate to Oxford Circus, and Metroline's route 390 was extended from Marble Arch to Notting Hill Gate. On Guy Fawkes' Day Friday 5th November, many guest vehicles turned out for the last crew day on the 12, some of them re-creating workings through to long-gone former terminals as far apart as

South Croydon and Harlesden. The familiar 'Commercial Services' RM 9 and RML 2725 duly ran in on the last crew journeys. A feature of this conversion was that, as the 12 was one of the '24-hour' services with the same type of bus day and night, the first bendy-buses started work late at night on 5th before the last Routemasters had returned to the garage.

In the previous few weeks, many of the RMs were re-registered to allow the traditional original registrations to be retained for re-sale by the company. Large numbers of RMs and RMLs were soon sold to Ensign Bus who by this time were amassing quite a large stock. On Sunday 5th December Ensign Bus staged a grand 'Routemaster Raffle' whereby 32 people had successfully bid for a chance to buy a Routemaster at a knock-down price. Although a handful of Arriva buses were included, most of those driven away on that day were RMLs that had been released from route 12.

RM 2051 Oxford Street
RMLs 2335 and 2273
Walworth Road
RML 2584 Camberwell

CAPITAL TRANSPORT

DAVID JACKMAN

Piccadilly – the Last Stronghold

At the beginning of
2005 four busy routes
still served the length
of Piccadilly with
Routemasters.

2005

At the start of 2005, just routes 13, 14, 19, 22, 36, 38 and 159 remained with Routemasters, but with not far short of 200 buses between them. Although the fates of the 19 and 36 were sealed already, the others had a long while to go before their contracts expired and the operators concerned were reluctant to buy new buses without guarantees of contract extensions. Nevertheless, TfL and the Mayor wanted all Routemasters, and indeed all 'non accessible' buses, to go from normal service by the end of 2005, so it was only a matter of time before the matter was resolved.

Route 36, which had featured in the partial conversion back in February 2003, was the first to be fully converted to opo buses, from 29th January 2005. The existing contract, which ran until 27th May 2007, was merely modified for the type and mode change. In the end sixteen guest vehicles turned out on the last crew day, and once again RM 9 fulfilled its customary role as the last crew bus. Although several of the RMLs moved over to Putney to replace some defective examples, some of the RMLs and all of the RMs quickly passed to Ensign Bus.

STEPHEN MADDEN

KIM RENNIE

On Sunday 27th February, one week before several routes changed hands in east London, First ran special journeys over routes 97, 123 and 158, all of which were to pass to Stagecoach from 5th March. Silver RM 1650 (SRM 3), red RML 2735 with its LT fleetname and open-top RMC 1510 (in spite of the freezing weather that day!) operated many journeys on a complicated schedule over ten hours. On Friday 4th March Stagecoach did a similar operation, with RML 2665 in national livery, supported by Blue Triangle's RM 298 and Sullivan's RM 1069 as well as Titan T 1, all running on route 58, a service that First was to take

over on the following day. Later in the year, First used their 'heritage fleet' of four Routemasters on special occasions, for example in July and August on extra Green Line journeys between London and Windsor. Go-Ahead featured again between 5th and 8th April when they loaned RML 2725 to Brighton & Hove, who used it in that city on their routes 5/5A. By now, the Commercial Services fleet of London Central and General had five operational Routemasters in its fleet, RM 9 and RMLs 2283, 2604, 2725 and 2732. DRM 2516 had been withdrawn and its platform doors were donated to RML 2283.

RML 2578 Vauxhall
RM 1980 Royal Oak
RML 2676 Camberwell

57

Last bell sounds for No 19 as Ken goes back on his word

At the terminus: the much-loved Finsbury Park to Battersea Bridge bus will join the others that have been withdrawn

The disappearing Routemasters

73 Tottenham
13 Golders Green
Archway
390
Finsbury Park
19
38 Clapton
Hackney
98 Willesden
Queens Park
Swiss Cottage
Islington
6 Kensal Park
36 Kilburn
Camden
Bethnal Green
8 Bow
23
King's Cross
Liverpool Street 11
East Acton 7
Paddington
Notting Hill
Limehouse
Canning Town
94
Central London
Elephant & Castle
15 Blackwall
Acton Green
9 Kensington
10
Hammersmith
11
19
Fulham
Battersea
Clapham
137
New Cross
36
Peckham
12 Dulwich
14
22 Putney
Streatham
159

Routemaster routes still operating
Routemaster routes withdrawn
Route 19 disappearing today

BY ROSS LYDALL
Local Government Correspondent

ONE of London's best-loved Routemaster bus routes will begin to disappear today.

The 19, which links Finsbury Park to Battersea, is being converted to new low-floor double-deckers.

This leaves conductors and the 50-year-old buses on only five routes. All remaining 140 jump-on, jump-off vehicles will be gone by November under Ken Livingstone's demand for an "accessible" bus fleet.

This is despite remarks by the Mayor, made in 2001 and unearthed this week, that "only some ghastly dehumanised moron would want to get rid of the Routemasters".

But it comes as Transport for London (TfL) confirmed a "heritage bus" service using Routemasters will begin operating within months around central London.

Routemaster enthusiasts said it was ironic that the 19 was being withdrawn on April Fools' Day.

Ben Brook, of the Save the Routemaster campaign, said: "TfL is laughing in the face of Londoners by removing the Routemasters on the 19. It's one of the most loved routes in London and proof that TfL don't give a stuff about Londoners' wishes."

The last Routemaster on the 19

will leave Finsbury Park station at 12.15am tomorrow. Bus operator Arriva will make 44 of the 75 conductors redundant, while the rest will be retrained and remain within the company. Almost half the 28 Routemasters used on the route will be sold off.

This will leave Routemasters operating on the 13, 14, 22, 38 and 159 routes. Less than two years ago there were 500 Routemasters on 20 routes, including 49 buses bought and refurbished by TfL following the Mayor's manifesto pledge to bring back conductors.

The 14 and 22 will convert to low-floor double deckers on 22 July, while the 38 will become a bendy-bus route shortly afterwards. Details of the heritage route are

being ironed out, but there was a formal tender in which TfL invited firms to bid for a new service for "principal tourist attractions in the central London area".

A TfL spokesman said: "We have got proposals from several operators. We are considering these now with a view to introducing heritage services during the summer."

Details of the heritage bus plan were revealed by TfL in response to a freedom of information request by the Evening Standard.

Andrew Morgan, chairman of the Routemaster Association, said: "It's a great shame they couldn't keep an actual route within the network."

EDITORIAL COMMENT: PAGE 13

'Only some ghastly dehumanised moron would want to get rid of the Routemasters'

— Ken Livingstone, 2001

Driving us round the bend: the newer bendy bus has been shown to make far more noise than the Routemaster, right, that it is replacing

New buses noisier than Routemaster

SCRAPPING the Routemaster bus and replacing it with a modern fleet is inflicting even more noise on Londoners, a new survey reveals.

Newer buses are so much noisier, experts say it is like turning up the volume from "medium to high".

The iconic double-decker remains on only six routes because Transport for London wants the city's 7,000-strong bus fleet to be fully accessible to disabled people.

The remaining 170 Routemasters will go by the end of the year in a move criticised by campaigners who want to save them. Tests conducted for the Evening Standard, however, reveal that the new bendy bus blasts passers-by with 92.1 decibels of noise from the engine, tyres and exhaust.

Experts say it is the equivalent of standing at the back of a live rock concert.

By contrast the Routemaster — in service since 1954 — was measured at a comparatively muffled 89.6 decibels.

All other new buses in the capital and surveyed by the UK Noise Association and Transport 2000 are also louder than the Routemaster.

The average noise emitted by a new single-decker is 93.4 decibels. Researchers using noise-measuring equipment found that a modern double-decker is louder too; on average emitting 90.6 decibels of sound.

All modern buses surveyed were as loud as or noisier than a black cab which was recorded at 90.6 decibels.

Today the Noise Association said that hundreds of new buses were having a "significant" impact on noise levels in the capital. John Stewart, of the UK Noise Association, said: "Ironically, with the Mayor's push to get more buses on London's roads — which is a laudable move — it is now making a significant difference to noise levels we all experi-

BY DAVID WILLIAMS
Motoring Editor

ence. It is very disappointing that new vehicles are actually noisier than those produced 50 years ago."

Mr Stewart added: "While car manufacturers have been under pressure to produce quieter vehicles with lower emissions it seems buses have been left behind because of their 'cuddly' image."

World Health Organisation guidelines say that any continuous noise above 55 decibels can be enough to cause "serious annoyance". The noisiest single vehicle discovered in Victoria was a modern double-decker recorded at 104 decibels.

However, the noisiest group of vehicles were large lorries which averaged 94.8 decibels.

All bus readings far outweighed the noise generated by cars, which averaged only 88.1 decibels and white vans which were recorded at 88.6 decibels. The quietest vehicle was the small lorry — marginally quieter in most cases than the family car. Three-tonne trucks sent the noise meter's needle to 88 decibels on average. Motorbikes average 93.5 decibels, roughly the same as a single-decker bus.

Andrew Morgan, vice president of the Routemaster Association, said: "Despite all the supposed engineering advances, new buses in London are not only noisier; they are more uncomfortable and heavier. The transport experience is not getting better."

A spokesman for Transport for London said: "The new buses are far cleaner. They meet stringent emissions regulations ... they carry more passengers as well as being accessible for the disabled."

HOW THEY RANK

	Average volume in decibels
Large lorry	94.8
Motorcycle	93.5
Single-decker bus	93.4
Large delivery van	92.8
Bendy bus	92.1
Scooter/moped	92
Modern double-decker	90.6
Black cab	90.6
Routemaster bus	89.6
Petrol car	88.1
Small lorry	88

Next it was the turn of the 19 to be converted. Set for 2nd April, the contract renewal date was brought forward from the due date of 30th April. There was a problem in that Battersea Garage is very small (it could just about accommodate the Routemasters) but the replacement buses were longer and the pvr was higher, and required some of the new buses to be outstationed at Norwood. A dozen guest vehicles helped out on the last crew day on Friday 1st, and RML 2347 became the last of the based buses to run in to Battersea. Again, Arriva's own RMLs were sent to Ensign Bus, but some of those RMLs owned by TfL were immediately sold off, mainly because there was nowhere to store them. Twelve of the refurbished RMs, which included the six that had been dealt with by Arriva themselves, were kept back for continued use on route 159.

Routes 14 and 22 both had contracts lasting beyond 2005. The 14 had been the last route to be re-awarded (in April 2002) for continuing Routemaster operation from 23rd November 2002 for at least five years and possibly for seven. The 22 had its last contract renewed from 22nd July 2000, in this case for seven years and also for

Routemasters. By early 2005, it was evident that pressure was there to convert both routes to driver only operation. An order for new Volvo B7TLs was placed by February, and in due course these arrived in time for a conversion of both services from 23rd July 2005. In June, Putney Garage's lowest numbered RML, 887, was repainted to pre-war General livery of red and white with black relief and silver roof, and it worked on the 14 and 22 until the conversion date, ending up as the last crew bus in on route 14. Although the familiar RM 9 appeared in service on the 22 on the last crew day, it was RML 2466 that performed the last journey, having replaced the intended 2640. An interesting aside to the Putney fleet is that a few of them had spent much of their life at the garage, and 2466 had been there for all but five of its forty years of service. RML 2590 beat that, though, being unique in that it had only ever run from Putney. It had been first allocated there in November 1966 when the 14 was upgraded from RM to RML, and after each overhaul had returned there. RML 887 was retained in the Commercial Services fleet, but once again most of the redundant RMLs were soon sold off to Ensign Bus.

Over
RML 2290 Putney
RML 2637 Fulham
RML 2502 Fulham
RML 2520 Brompton Road
RML 2669 Piccadilly
RML 2262 Harrods

RML 2531 Angel

DAVID JACKMAN

COLIN STANNARD

COLIN STANNARD

Over
RML 2612
Lower Richmond Road
RML 899 Kings Road
RML 2590 New Kings Road
RML 2615 Parsons Green

After the Putney conversion, just three crew routes remained, although the fates of all of them had been formulated by this time. The total pvr was exactly 100, of which 19 were on route 13, 50 on the 38 and 31 on the 159. Route 13 was in a similar category as the 14 and 22 in that its last contract renewal was from 1st September 2001, in this case for five years and utilising RMs owned by TfL. Due to be re-offered to tender in the summer of 2005, it was necessary to secure at least a two-year extension to the contract. Approval for this came by April 2005, new Scania buses were ordered and a driver-only conversion date was set for 22nd October 2005. Route 38 also had a five-year contract with Routemasters, which had begun on 20th July 2002. However, in December 2004 proposals were issued with the intention to convert the route to articulated single-deck operation in the autumn of 2005. In March 2005 Citaros were ordered, delivery began in July and the conversion date was set for 29th October.

RM 329 Golders Green
RM 1735 Baker Street
RM 1018 Finchley Road

CAPITAL TRANSPORT

Once again, suitable garage accommodation was a problem. In this case, TfL stepped in early with a stated intention to move their East Thames Buses operation out of Ash Grove Garage at Hackney later in the year. This was so that, if necessary, Ash Grove could be used by Arriva for the 38.

CAPITAL TRANSPORT

RM 659 Golders Green

The 13 was one of those routes that converted to opo during the evening anyway, and so the last Routemasters came off during the Friday evening of 21st October. The customary guest vehicles ran during the day as did RM 1562, unique in the London Sovereign fleet in having a white relief band and a Euro-3 engine. It had been expected that 1562 would work the last crew journey but, in the event, RM 1005 took over running number BT17 by the evening peak. There were large crowds about on this 'last day' and there was considerable interest from the local people and press. The last RM was duplicated by London United's RML 880 and Blue Triangle's RT 3871 and RTW 75. Some of the redundant RMs had been earmarked by TfL for the 'heritage routes' and some left Edgware Garage that evening with almost indecent haste. Others were sent to storage on behalf of TfL at Tolworth Garage.

CAPITAL TRANSPORT

CAPITAL TRANSPORT

CAPITAL TRANSPORT

66

One week later it was the turn of the 38 and again it was notable for the number of local people and ordinary passengers that were aware of the conversion to 'bendy buses' and who were taking their last rides (and photographs) of the Routemasters. A greater number of guest vehicles appeared on Friday 28th, star items including RMF 1254 and Bristol K6A HLJ 44. The RMF was making its very first appearance on London bus service (it had been a demonstrator and with BEA when new) and the Bristol K was a vehicle that when new in 1949 had worked on hire with LT. Cobham Bus Museum had provided STL 2377 on special private runs on the 'last crew days' of the 19, 14 and 13 but on the 38 they sent 'Tilling' ST 922. The very last crew bus on the 38 was RML 888 as CT131, finally getting back to Clapton Garage at 0230, around an hour late, and with several duplicate buses from Blue Triangle running ahead. Nine of the RMs passed to the 'heritage routes', others went into storage (some at Tolworth with those from the 13), whilst the bulk of the redundant RMLs went to Arriva's Tottenham Marshes storage depot, and most duly went to Ensign.

Meanwhile, special operations continued to occur. First's RML 2735 worked some journeys on route 258 in the Harrow area on 29th October, as a kind of commemoration to the route being lost to another operator in February 2006. On Friday 11th November, it was the last day of First on route 27 and of London United on the 33. First's silver SRM 3 duly worked several journeys on the 27 and LU's historic liveried RML 880 came out for two round trips on the 33 between Fulwell and Barnes. These operations seemed to indicate, even though mainstream Routemaster operation was almost at an end, that the occasional celebratory workings would still feature a Routemaster or two. Indeed, even after the 159 conversion, on 23rd December Metroline's RML 903 and Blue Triangle's RT 3062 on route 4 commemorated what was the last day of step-entrance buses on mainstream everyday TfL services, thus achieving the Mayor's wish for universal operation of low floor accessible buses. In each of these examples, and as had become customary, fares and donations collected all went to nominated charities.

JAMES LIDSEY

PHILIPPA SPRATT

KIM RENNIE

CAPITAL TRANSPORT
CAPITAL TRANSPORT

The 159 thus found itself in the position of the last mainstream Routemaster route in London. It had been due to be re-offered to tender by March 2005 for a renewal in February 2006 in the normal course of events. To make sure that it could lose its crew buses before the end of 2005, in turn to agree with the Mayor's intentions to remove all non-accessible buses by that date, it was offered to tender several months early. In an unusually speedy award, on 31st January 2005 it was awarded back to Arriva but with an open-ended start date 'by the end of the year.' New buses were ordered in March, but delivery could not be assured until October and November. A conversion from crew to driver-only operation was set for 10th December 2005 which was actually carried out during the 9th.

IAN BELL

CAPITAL TRANSPORT

CAPITAL TRA

KIM RENNIE

MARK KEHOE

Great Routemaster Journeys   James Whiting

ROUTE 38 *Clapton Pond to Victoria*
It is the Saturday before route 38 loses its
Routemasters. Next Saturday, bendy buses
take over. I have decided to spend the
afternoon travelling on the route and start
my journey in Lower Clapton Road, two
stops from the Clapton Pond terminus, a
small green oasis in a built-up inner city
area. I will not be staying on the same bus
for the whole journey as I am aiming to
meet up with route 38's Duke Baysee at
some point. Duke was featured in an
Evening Standard article on Wednesday.
Apparently he is in the habit of playing
reggae music to his passengers on the har-
monica. Whilst this musical combination
would not normally appeal to me, hearing it
on a Routemaster in service would have a
novelty value (so long as it's only once). No
luck on the first bus to arrive but I get on
and sit downstairs at the front.

We pass through Hackney and then past
the future Dalston Junction station of the
East London Line extension to reach the
Balls Pond Road. At the bus stop near its
junction with Kingsland Road, a young man
in a bright red uniform can be seen handing
out leaflets about the forthcoming introduc-
tion of bendy buses and chatting with a
passenger at the bus stop. I don't know
exactly what they are saying but the passenger has a sceptical look on her face and
the young man a look of quiet resignation.
The new roadside ticket machines are
installed in readiness to come into service
next week.

MARK KEHOE

Passengers mourn as the 38 bus goes bendy

BY ANDREW GILLIGAN
on the No 38 bus

Passengers mourn as the 38 bus goes bendy

BY ANDREW GILLIGAN
on the No 38 bus

IT WAS the bus that once took Tony Blair (and thousands of less famous Islington-dwellers) to work.

But today, passengers on the No 38 are mourning the final departure of their beloved Routemasters as the service is turned over to TfL's controversial bendy buses.

At 1.24am tonight the last Routemaster will pull in o the 38's Clapton terminus, bringing the bus to the edge of extinction in London.

Only one route, the 159, will remain Routemaster-operated for the next six weeks. After that, apart from a few tourist services, the iconic vehicle's 50-year journey through the capital will be at an end.

"Everybody I know hates the bendy buses," said Margaret Bacon of Hackney. "They've put them on the 73 and you see people in the morning hanging back to get on the Routemaster behind."

Enthusiasts and mourners were out in force along the route last night and today, with more than 20 special journeys by "guest buses" scheduled to run.

Dozens of people waited with cameras to take souvenir pictures and there was widespread anger towards TfL and the Mayor. "They promised to save these buses a few years back," said Thomas Allen, a banker from Islington. "Why have they have broken that promise?"

But not everyone will be mourning the Routemasters' demise.

The Mayor pointed out that two people had died getting off them in the past two years, while Bob Niven, chief executive of the Disability Rights Commission, said: "Accessible buses have transformed the lives of thousands of disabled Londoners.

"The question is not whether we are for or against Routemasters, but whether everyone should be able to use public transport."

EVENING STANDARD 28/10/05

The Balls Pond Road, of all places, is in the process of becoming 'gentrified' and identical Victorian terraced houses can be seen both in run-down condition and in fully restored state with white painted exteriors, tastefully painted front doors and brass fittings. It is at No.87 that, in the local dialects, the road name changes from Baws Pon Rowd to Bowls Pawned Rowed, only to change back to Baws Pon Rowd at No.159. These dividing lines will probably have changed by the time you read this of course, as a number of newly arrived estate agents are having a field day.

The journey continues on another RML and I ask the conductor how long he has been conducting. '26 years, at seven different garages,' is his reply. 'And next week?' 'Oh, I won't be looking for another job; I'm at retirement age.' I ask him if he has seen Duke Baysee. 'He's still with us, but I haven't seen him today.'

We approach Islington, parts of which are fully gentrified now. There is a point on the 38 route just north of Islington Green where there is a sudden change from old Islington with its cheaper and rented properties to café society Islington, with its coffee houses, bars and antique shops. At the stop near Angel station some local yobs have smashed a large pane of glass in one of the bus shelters. Some new-intake locals with a sense of civic pride are helping to clear up shards of glass from the pavement.

The 38 then travels down Rosebery Avenue, past Sadlers Wells theatre where Shaolin monks are performing Kung Fu acrobatics, and Finsbury Town Hall with its elaborate Victorian entrance awning. I get off in Bloomsbury and watch a few 38s travel by, still looking for the reggae player. No sighting, but I decide to hop on RM 1640 at the bus stop outside Conway Hall. As I do so a young woman sitting on the off-side bench seat is videotaping passengers getting on and off the bus. The RM travels on with a fairly healthy load and the bus conductor in a multicoloured woolly hat roves around collecting fares and checking passes. Once again I have managed to get the front seat downstairs and when the seat opposite becomes free the woman with the video camera moves to it to interview three elderly ladies sitting behind me. She is making a video about the Routemaster bus for a college project.

'Why do you think they are getting rid of them?' the interviewer asks. 'Well, they're getting old aren't they. They probably don't make them anymore'. 'They're expensive to run,' offers another lady, 'they need a driver and a conductor'. The third interviewee raises the accessibility factor. 'Do you remember them when they were new?' 'Oh yes, they were the latest thing when I was your age'. This is probably the sort of thing that a pensioner says to a teenager about almost anything that has been around since their youth, but my own recollection is that such enthusiasm in the 1950s and 1960s was limited to people like me and 55 Broadway. I vividly recall sharing my first sighting of RM 1 in 1957, when it passed our flat in NW10 one day whilst out of service. I ran into the sitting room excitedly announcing that I had just seen the new bus design. 'What new bus design?' was the response. 'Like this,' I replied, showing my mother and a neighbour a drawing of RM 1 that I had cut out of a 1956 edition of the Beezer comic. 'But they're all like that,' was their reply. And thus, at the tender age of eight, I was faced with a moment of shocking realisation: I had been born into a family and a community that were unable to see much difference between an RT and an RM. I was subsequently to discover that this was a common problem in society, but I don't think I will ever fully fathom how I overcame this early bus-related trauma to develop into a well balanced and rational human being fully able to enjoy riding around on buses for fun and standing in the road photographing them.

The interview with the trio of pensioners was completed just as we entered Victoria station. Journey completed, the interviewer and I could not help noticing the RML parked in front of us on the stand. A large band of rock musicians in black leather – we counted twelve – were boarding, complete with guitar cases, keyboards and an amplifier. Typical. You wait around for a musician and then twelve turn up together. The conductor waves them off the bus, so they try to get on RM 1640. Now, anyone with any common sense would realise that if you cannot fit the equipment for a 12-piece rock band on an RML, there would be even less chance on an RM, so I can only assume that the difference had escaped the attention of the band. The conductor of RM 1640 has gone off somewhere, so they are making good progress despite deciding to go upstairs. By now, however, they have attracted the attention of the 38 Route Controller. 'Where are you going with all this stuff?' he enquires. 'Tottenham Court Road,' is the reply. 'Not on this, you're not.

You can use the 73 bendy bus; that's what they're for'.

The rock musicians transfer to the bendy bus without quibble despite having humped quite a lot of gear on to the RM's upper deck. By now I am quite engrossed in the whole affair and I follow the musicians to the 73. I have a brief chat with one of them. Apparently the twelve musicians are two rock bands travelling together. They have come over from Germany, which probably explains why they so readily obeyed the man in the uniform.

I feel as though I have been present at a historic moment: the last time twelve heavy metal musicians attempt to smuggle their orchestras on board a Routemaster on the 38. It could even be a first. I have a brief chat with the 38 Route Controller afterwards. 'Have you ever seen twelve rock musicians trying to get on an RM with their instruments before,' I ask. 'No, never,' he replies convincingly. I also ask if he has seen Duke Baysee today, but he hasn't. Perhaps it's his day off.

ROUTE 159 *Streatham to Marble Arch*
Oxford Street on the last Saturday of
Routemasters on the 159 is busy with
Christmas shoppers. It is a mild day for 3rd
December and the street is packed with
Christmas shoppers. It is just before 4pm
and beginning to get dark as I hop on RML
2545 near Oxford Circus to go to Streatham
Station. There are six standing passengers
downstairs and a few standing upstairs.
After I get on the conductor declares the bus
full. Our progress towards Piccadilly Circus is
slow as traffic is heavy, but soon a few people get off and I and others get seats. Below
the windows on the lower deck, the original
maroon now appears as the moquette
applied during major refurbishment has
been removed. Upstairs, as I discovered later
in the trip, light grey is the colour.

Like most of the other Routemasters on
the 159, RML 2545's exterior advertising
spaces are now devoted to publicising the
two recently introduced heritage routes.
Inside, a series of six posters above each
row of windows mentions an aspect of
Routemaster history in each decade of its
life. I had expected to see more bus enthusiasts riding around on the 159 today, but
see only two obvious bus fans on my round
trip. Without wishing to be unkind, I have to
say that the passengers on the bus are a
pretty miserable looking bunch. One of
them has the facial expression of a man
that a compassionate beggar might offer
some money to. Perhaps they are under the
mistaken belief that the 159 is being converted to bendy buses.

The journey in the Streatham direction is
uneventful, though the poor condition of
Streatham Hill and the suspension on the
RML give a very bumpy ride. I imagine a
tram in its latter days descending the same
hill on poorly maintained track. Route 159
turns round in the specially provided turning circle alongside the one-time Streatham
bus garage. This garage was completely
rebuilt in the mid-1980s only to be closed
five years after reopening as a result of
privatisation. The former garage is now in
use as a covered go-kart track and – out of
respect no doubt – one of the curves on the
track is named in honour of the former
bus wash.

I walk to the first 159 bus stop to begin my journey over the complete route to Marble Arch. RML 2730 pulls up as I reach the stop. It has very screechy brakes and, inside, very worn seats. When we reach heavy traffic in the northern half of Streatham High Road, the brakes are on almost continuously for a time and the high pitched sound they give out occasionally resembles someone playing a penny whistle rather badly, the subtlest change of pressure on the brake pedal resulting in a change of pitch. This creates some fascination outside the bus as well.

We reach the Brixton shopping area with its Christmas illuminations. It is about 6pm and I get off 2730 to photograph the recently rebuilt frontage of Brixton Underground station, impressively floodlit at night. Brixton is a colourful and lively place but with a well-known dark side. Just around the corner from where I stand, various substances can be bought that would make the illuminations even more impressive, perhaps even with the power to bring smiles to the faces of passengers on the 159, but I decide to wait for the next Routemaster instead.

The next 159 turns out to be going only as far as Kennington Park Post Office according to the destination blind, although as would become clear a little later, no-one else getting on the bus notices this. It also happens to be RM 29, one of the most recent refurbishments and still in very nice condition. I do not know where Kennington Park Post Office is, but this looks like an opportunity to find out.

RM 29 sets off for this mysterious destination in heavy traffic at first but we pick up speed half way up Brixton Road, where smart Georgian terraced houses take over from less attractive buildings.

We continue up Kennington Road away from Kennington towards Waterloo. It is not until we get near Lambeth North Station, where Kennington Road meets Lambeth Road, that the conductor shouts out 'Last stop'. The response from the passengers on the lower deck is 'Last stop???' in a high-pitched three-question-mark tone of voice reminiscent of a Monty Python sketch. The conductor correctly points out that the blinds show Kennington Park but resists the temptation to tell us about the extra mile or so we have travelled beyond it. I assume the point we have travelled to is not on the blinds and later learn that Kennington Park is opposite Oval tube station; the bus stop at which we have been set down is marked 'Imperial War Museum'.

It is now about 6.30 and beginning to get a bit chilly so I am pleased when RM 1124 turns up with Marble Arch as its desti-nation. RM 1124 (right) is in the red interior style, never having been fully refurbished. Its tungsten lights have been replaced with fluorescent lights at some point in its life, but not the full length versions, and the seats have been recovered in the moquette used for the early 1990s modernisation of the fleet. It still retains an 'original' air about it, though very tatty by now. It certainly feels more original than the refurbished bus we pass at Trafalgar Square on the newly introduced 'heritage route' 9. It would have been nice if some of the buses from the 159, many of which have the original winding windows, could have been used – and I understand the operators felt the same – but we must be thankful for small mercies.

Traffic has eased a bit by the time we get to the West End and our journey along Oxford Street is not too slow. At the traffic lights opposite Selfridges, three girls in their twenties get on. 'We're only going one stop,' says the conductor. 'That's OK,' one of them replies. She then excitedly tells the other two that 'This is an old, old Routemaster, nice and cosy – I do miss these buses'. She has dragged her two friends on board for a short ride on a treas-ured childhood memory. At last I have seen a smiling face on a 159, even if only for about 300 yards.

Last Day Guests

David Stewart

The phenomenon of the 'guest vehicle' coming to help to commemorate the passing of crew operation at each stage of the conversion programme gradually took hold, with many familiar vehicles appearing but with several that had not been seen in PSV service for many a year. Some of the 'guests' were actually members of the incumbent companies' so-called heritage fleets, kept back mainly for private hire work. In each route conversion, it became the norm for any fares or donations taken on the guest vehicles to go to a nominated charity, and TfL agreed to waive their receipt of fares on these occasions.

The first two partial RM conversions on the 10 and 36 in early 2003 were not marked in this way, but it was Stagecoach

and the 15 in August 2003 that started the trend. The first 'surprise' appeared in the shape of RML 2456 newly repainted into Country Area green. More notable 'specials' followed, examples including RTW 75 on the 8, Saunders bodied roof-box RT 3062 on the 12, Cravens RT 1431 on the 36 and RLH 61 on the 22. The first two were with Blue Triangle and the latter two with Ensign, and all four were after long-term restorations back to PSV status, appearing again on later occasions. Ensign made a bit of a name for itself for 'surprises' and two more first-timers ran, first on the 38 and later on the 159. RMF 1254 was hired from Imperial Buses and made history in that it was the first time that it had worked in 'LT' service; when new it had been a demonstrator and was then with BEA and Northern General. The other was HLJ44, a green Bristol K6A that had actually ran on loan to LT in 1949, albeit in the country area even though similar examples had indeed run on the 38 at that time. The last restoration of all was RT 624, also by Ensign, who ran it on the 159; the vehicle was restored to its 1979 condition to recall its status as the last RT to work route 62 in that year.

Additionally, the LT Museum's FRM 1 made a very rare foray on the 73 and RM 1, the first Routemaster of all, worked a few journeys on some of the 'last days' And then there was Cobham Bus Museum: although their RTL 139 and RML 3 worked occasionally, after September 2004 this no longer happened. Instead, even more spectacular workings occurred when the restored 1937-vintage STL 2377 performed 'photographers' specials' with invited guests aboard over parts of routes 19, 14 and 13, and the even older ST 922 followed on the 38 and 159. Also on the 38's 'last day' privately owned RTs 190 and 191 were posed at various points for photographers and these were authorised to do so.

Various privately owned vehicles featured in service occasionally, but after the route 12 conversion in November 2004 there was a change of TfL policy. Henceforth, only Class-6 MoT vehicles on the Operators Licences of TfL-approved contractors were allowed. Even so, privately owned RM 613 was a Class 6 and ran from then on under First's licence, and was joined on the 159 by RTW 467 in a similar category. Occasionally, and especially during the 159 'last days', a few other vehicles travelled over the routes outside formal service with only owners and/or invited guests on board. However, one or two private vehicles (e.g. RF 48 on the 22, RMC 1456 on the 38 and ICL's RML 2727 on the 159) did not conform to the rules or were unaware of them, and ran along the routes displaying blinds or boards. The well-known RT 1702, after being able to operate on some 'last days' was unable to do so after November 2004, but instead ran along some of the routes (36/A/B, 19, 14, 38 and 159) with front blinds dropped down and only with invited passengers aboard.

Authorised Guest and Special Vehicles

Route 15 – RT 3871, RTL 139, RMC 1456, RMC 1461, RML 2456.
Route 11 – RM 9.
Route 23 – RT 4421, RM 613, RML 2456.
Route 94 – RML 880.
Routes 6 and 98 (each ran on both routes) – RT 3871, RMC 1513, RML 2456, M 1.
Route 8 – RT 1702, RT 1790, RT 3232, RT 3871, RT 4421, RTL 139, RTW 75, RTW 467, RM 1, RM 5, RM 8, RM 298, RMC 1456, RMC 1461, RMC 1469, RML 900, RML 2456, RML 2665, RML 2760, SRM 3, M 1, T 1, T 2.
Route 7 – RT 3871, RTL 139, RTW 75, RM 1, RM 120, RM 613, RM 938, RMC 1510, RML 2313, RML 2735, SRM 3.
Route 137 – RT 1702, RM 642, RM 2217.
Route 9 – RT 3871, RTL 139, RTW 75, RML 3, RM 9, RM 1069, RMC 1469, RML 2665, SRM 3.
Route 390 (also as 10) – RT 786, RT 3871, RML 903, RMC 1513, RML 2310, M 1.
Route 73 – RT 4421, RTL 139, RTW 75, RTW 467, RM 1, RML 3, RM 5, RM 25, RM 613, RM 1000, RM 2217, RML 2524, RML 2665, RCL 2220, FRM 1, SRM 3, VA 115.
Route 12 – RT 1702, RT 3062, RT 3871, RT 4421, RM 613, RM 642, RML 900, RCL 2220, RML 2405, SRM 3.
Route 36 – RT 1431, RT 3062, RT 3871, RT 4421, RTW 75, RM 1, RM 5, RM 9, RM 25, RM 613, RML 900, RML 2317, RML 2405, RML 2665, SRM 3.
Route 19 – RT 1431, RT 3062, RT 3871, RT 4421, RM 5, RM 613, RML 2272, RML 2317, RML 2665, RMA 58, VA 115.
Route 14 – RT 1431, RT 4421, RTW 75, RML 887.
Route 22 – RT 1431, RTW 75, RM 9, RML 2317, RLH 61.
Route 13 – RT 3871, RT 4421, RTW 75, RM 9, RM 613, RML 880, RML 903, RML 2665, RML 2735, RLH 61.
Route 38 – RT 1431, RT 3062, RT 3871, RT 4421, RTW 75, RM 5, RM 6, RM 298, RM 613, RML 900, RMF 1254, RML 2665, RML 2760, SRM 3, RLH 61, HLJ44.
Route 159 – RT 624, RT 1431, RT 3062, RT 3232, RT 3871, RT 4421, RTW 75, RTW 467, RM 1, RM 5, RM 6, RM 613, RMF 1254, RMC 1453, RM 2217, RCL 2220, RCL 2260, RML 2317, RML 2405, RML 2565, RML 2665, RML 2760, RLH 61, HLJ44.

Additional vehicles not authorised to carry passengers on TfL services (post-November 2004), but which ran along the lines of route, carrying some passengers free of charge. Note that RT 1702 and RMC 1456 had run in service prior to November 2004 with suitable authorisation.

RF 48 – 22.
RT 1702 – 36/A/B, 19, 14, 38, 159.
RMC 1456 – 38.
RML 2727 – 159.

Vehicles on photographic runs carrying invited guests only.
STL 2377 (Cobham Bus Museum) – 19, 14, 13.
ST 922 (Cobham Bus Museum) – 38, 159.
RTs 190 and 191 (private owners) – 38.

MARK KEHOE

MARK KEHOE

MARTIN RUTHE

CAPITAL TRANSPORT

STEVE MASKELL

CAPITAL TRANSPORT

CAPITAL TRANSPORT

KEVIN SMITH

KEVIN SMITH

KIM RENNIE

KIM RENNIE

KEVIN SMITH

CAPITAL TRANSPORT

KEVIN SMITH

COLIN STANNARD

COLIN STANNARD

STEVE MASKELL

STEVE MASKELL

STEPHEN MADDEN

JOHN BRADSHAW

MARK KEHOE

CAPITAL TRANSPORT

Goodbye Old Friend

The final 159 schedule, which had been marginally increased from 2nd April 2005, called for a pvr of 31 buses on Monday-Friday, 24 on Saturday and 13 on Sunday, serviced by a final fleet of 36 Routemasters (13 RMs and 23 RMLs). These included the six refurbished by Arriva in 2003/4.

The guest vehicle running day was on Thursday 8th December, the last full day of Routemasters on the 159. A fine array of twenty-four guest vehicles was to be seen. This was largely achieved by several of the 'guest runnings' being operated by different vehicles, swapped over on succeeding journeys. On the last day itself, Friday 9th, the normal service Routemasters were taken off during the middle of the day and replaced one-for-one by new Volvo B7TLs. The last two southbound RMLs vied for position, RML 2491 (BN139) left Marble Arch first, with RML 2387 (BN140) following five minutes later. By the time Brixton Hill had been reached they had swapped positions. 2387 reached Brixton Garage first at 1.12pm, allowing 2491 to set down its passengers at 1.13pm, thus becoming the last RML in service by a whisker. About an hour earlier, RML 2759 followed by RM 85 had been the last Routemasters to complete full northbound journeys to Marble Arch.

TfL arranged the 'very last RM run' and this was performed by RM 2217 (taking over running number BN143 from RM 85). It was the last standard length RM built in 1965 and had been newly repainted into standard Arriva livery but had not been used in service for some time. It left Marble Arch at 12.52 (the intended time was 12.10) for Brixton Garage, where it finally arrived at 2.03pm, and it was preceded by two other 'specials' in the Arriva fleet, the lowest numbered examples: RM 6 in gold, followed by RM 5 in red. All three buses were scheduled to terminate at the home garage. However, no-one had bargained for RM 54, working the last through journey to Streatham Garage. Although it had left Marble Arch much earlier than the 'specials', it somehow went slower and slower and by the time the others had reached Lambeth North Station it was between RMs 6 and 5 and only four minutes in front of RM 2217. They stayed in this sequence all the way to Brixton Garage. RM 54 went onward to Streatham, setting down opposite the old bus garage six minutes after RM 2217 set down its passengers.

On that last day, many people lined the route of the 159 cheering, waving and taking photographs as the last Routemasters passed by. London gave the bus a warm send off on a day that began foggy but turned to bright winter sunshine as the buses approached their final terminus.

112

STEPHEN MADDEN

STEPHEN MADDEN

PHIL WILLSON

RM 54 at the Streatham Station terminus shortly after RM 2217 had set down its passengers outside Brixton garage. Nigel Eadon-Clarke was on RM 54 and describes its historic journey.

I was at Marble Arch for much of the morning, but after around 11am 159s started going down Park Lane and stopping at the rear of the line of Big Bus Sightseeing vehicles. This made photography more difficult. Gold RM 6 was at the front of the layby with a couple of service buses behind and RM 5 then arrived and stopped at the back. Shortly afterwards I managed to get some good shots of RM 2217 as it arrived at Park Lane around 11.30am. It was difficult to know when to get on a bus to be sure of being able to get to Brixton on a Routemaster, but since RM 2217 was at Marble Arch it was time to leave. It was 11.40am and I hurried down to the first stop in Oxford Street (last bus was due to leave at around 12.10pm). People were already queuing past the first side road (there were approximately 120 people in front of me). A Routemaster appeared and there was a scramble, another appeared 10 mins later with the same scramble, but when it drove past me there were a lot of empty seats. This is when I and those around me realised that much of the queue was not interested in getting on a 'service' bus because they wanted to get on the last (not that there was any hope for most). Accordingly when the next one arrived, RM 54, I was able to get on and it still left with empty seats, the time now being around 12.20pm. The driver was excellent, going really slowly to allow people on every corner to take photos (and also I suspect to allow those buses behind to catch up). It was a joy to see everyone on the pavement smiling and waving together and taking thousands of camera shots. We reached Westminster at about 1.15pm and one other 159 had already overtaken us in Whitehall. The crowds on Westminster

Bridge meant we stopped and edged forward. By this time RM 5 was not far behind us and rumour had it that RM 2217 was in Whitehall. While we were stopped on the bridge, gold RM 6 overtook us and sped away. When we moved away from Westminster RM 5 was only a few yards behind us. Although we speeded up a bit after this there were still slow points at every major junction and people with cameras were always visible, along with many people using their mobile phone cameras to capture the moment. Near Brixton a primary school (Corpus Christi) had arranged for all the children to be on the pavement with flags and chants of '159' (see photo, page 115). As we passed Brixton station RM 5 was still visible behind.

Our bus was displaying Streatham Station, but we expected it to stop at Brixton garage for a changeover. Of course there were hundreds of people here and we stopped and edged forward. Was it going to terminate? No it went on; this led to a dilemma – should I get off or continue to Streatham Station. I decided to stay on because this could well become the last bus. It was certainly the 'last' to Streatham Station and on arrival the crew posed the bus opposite the old garage and stood in front for photos and signed tickets etc. The blind display had been set to 'NOT IN SERVICE' immediately on arrival, but the driver was persuaded to change it back to Streatham Station for more photographs. The bus then went on south out of service, to Norwood garage I believe. It had arrived at Streatham Station at 2.09pm (over one hour late). I wondered at the time whether it was the last in service, which was dependent on the time RM 2217 arrived at Brixton. By the time I got back to Brixton garage it was all over, but I had taken historic photos at Streatham and had ridden on the last Routemaster to this southern terminus.

It was subsequently confirmed that RM 2217 arrived at Brixton garage at 2.03pm so I was indeed among those on the last Routemaster in service on route 159, although this happened by pure chance. The conductor of RM 54 was asked what he was doing the following day and his answer was "I don't know". London will never be quite the same again.

159

You can still enjoy a ride on a Routemaster on Heritage Routes 9 & 15

HERITAGE ROUTES

Brixton Kennington
Westminster Whitehall
Trafalgar Sq Oxford St

STREATHAM STATION

You can still enjoy a ride on a Routemaster on Heritage Routes 9 & 15

HERITAGE ROUTES

159

LDS 279A

MARK KEHOE